This book belongs to:

Cooking is like love. It should be entered into with abandon or not at all.

–Harriet Van Horne

Gooseberry Patch
2500 Farmers Dr., #110
Columbus, OH 43235

www.gooseberrypatch.com
1•800•854•6673

Copyright 2011, Gooseberry Patch 978-1-936283-92-7
First Printing, May, 2011

Gooseberry Patch Co.®

Tiny Tips
for the
Kitchen

Dedication

*To everyone who knows
that the kitchen is
the heart of the home.*

*Life is uncertain.
Eat dessert first.*

–Ernestine Ulmer

Cupcakes for dessert tonight? Decorate them quickly
by dipping in frosting, then toss on some
chocolate chips or colored sprinkles just for fun.

For blue-ribbon perfect chocolate cakes
with no white streaks, use baking cocoa
instead of flour to dust greased pans.

Dress up a plain cake...lay a paper doily
on top, then sprinkle with powdered sugar or
baking cocoa. So dainty, yet so simple!

Create a pretty marbleized effect when baking a white cake mix. Simply sprinkle batter in its pan with a few drops of food coloring, then swirl the color around with a knife tip.

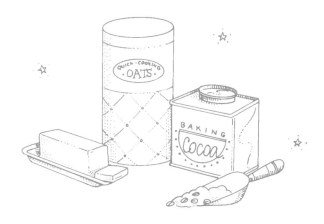

For best results, be sure to use the type of fat named
in the recipe. Butter bakes up well and gives cookies
wonderful flavor. Avoid light or whipped margarine
when baking. If shortening is called for, look for it
in easy-to-measure sticks.

Coffee adds a rich taste to chocolate recipes...just
substitute an equal amount for water or milk
in cake, cookie or brownie recipes.

To make a cake extra rich, substitute two egg yolks
for each whole egg.

Chopped or crushed candy bars make a fast & easy topping for frosted cakes. Try using toffee, caramel or nougat bars... mmm!

A long skewer or even a strand of spaghetti is useful in testing the doneness of deep cakes.

Save time when baking...tuck a measuring cup
into your countertop canisters. They are ready to
scoop out flour and sugar when you need them.

If you need just a little colored sugar for cookies and cupcakes, it's easy to make it yourself. Just place 1/4 cup of sugar in a small jar, add a drop or two of food coloring, cover the jar and shake to blend well. Spread the sugar on wax paper and let dry. Make some extra and store in an airtight container, and you'll have a rainbow of sugar ready for your next treat!

To create frosting in extra-bright, deep colors, check a craft or cake decorating supply store for paste-style food coloring.

Does a recipe call for toasted nuts or coconut? Toast your own by spreading in a shallow pan and baking at 350 degrees for 7 to 12 minutes, stirring frequently until golden.

Use an oven thermometer to check baking temperatures...no more burnt or underdone bread or cookies!

No peeking! When baking, the temperature drops 25 degrees every time the oven door is opened.

Parchment paper is a baker's best friend!
Place it on a baking sheet to keep cookies from spreading
and sticking...clean-up is a breeze too. Look for rolls of
parchment paper at groceries and bakery supply stores.

Warm cookies dipped in cold milk...one of life's simple pleasures.

–Unknown

For best results when baking cookies, allow butter and eggs to come to room temperature. Just set them out on the counter about an hour ahead of time and they'll be ready!

When baking in dark non-stick baking pans, set the oven temperature 25 degrees lower...baked goods won't overbrown.

If you're adding more than one baking pan to the oven, remember to stagger them on the racks. Placing one pan directly over another won't allow the food to cook evenly.

Before adding the brownie batter, line your baking dish with aluminum foil, then grease the foil. Once the brownies have baked and cooled, they'll lift right out of the pan.

Need a molasses substitution in a pinch?
Just use an equal measurement of honey.

Helpful to keep in mind: an equal amount of evaporated milk can be used if you don't have half-and-half in the fridge.

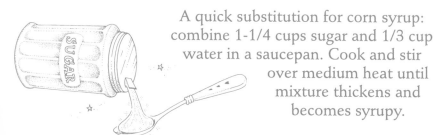

A quick substitution for corn syrup: combine 1-1/4 cups sugar and 1/3 cup water in a saucepan. Cook and stir over medium heat until mixture thickens and becomes syrupy.

Lighten up baked goods with ease! Applesauce can be used as a fat-free substitute for oil when baking cakes, muffins and other moist, cake-like goodies. Just substitute the same amount of applesauce as the recipe calls for oil.

Invite a young friend to bake with you!
Whether you're a basic baker or a master chef,
you're sure to have fun as you measure,
stir and sample together.

If you often use chopped onion, celery, carrots or green pepper to add flavor to sautéed dishes, save time by chopping lots at once. Create your own sauté blend and freeze it in a freezer-safe container. Add it to skillet dishes straight from the freezer…there's no need to thaw!

Keep mini pots of your favorite fresh herbs like oregano, chives, parsley and basil on a sunny kitchen windowsill...they'll be right at your fingertips for adding flavor to any dish!

To keep vegetables fresh and nutritious, wrap them in paper towels and store in unsealed plastic bags in the refrigerator.

Stock up on frozen vegetables when they go on sale. Flash-frozen soon after being harvested, they retain more nutrients than fresh produce that has traveled for several days before arriving in the grocery's produce aisle.

Buying boneless, skinless chicken breasts in bulk? Cook them all at once. Season with salt, pepper, and garlic, if desired, and allow to cool. Wrap tightly in plastic or place in a freezer bag. Kept in the freezer, they'll be ready for quick casseroles, sandwiches or zesty fajitas!

Freeze uncooked pork chops or chicken cutlets with marinade in freezer bags. After thawing overnight in the fridge, meat can go straight into the baking pan or skillet for a scrumptious meal in a jiffy!

Give a boost to recipes that use cream cheese by trying one that's flavored...chive, garlic, jalapeño or sun-dried tomato. Yummy!

It's simple to swap fresh for dried herbs! For one teaspoon of a dried herb, simply substitute one tablespoon of the fresh herb.

Did you know bread will stay freshest if it's stored on the counter, not refrigerated? For longer storage, drop it into a freezer bag and freeze for up to a month. Pop a frozen slice or two into the toaster for immediate use or let thaw at room temperature.

A spoonful of tomato paste adds rich flavor to stews and roasts. If you have a partial can left over, freeze the rest in ice cube trays, then pop out and store in a freezer bag. Frozen cubes can be dropped right into simmering dishes... there's no need to thaw!

*Cooking may be as much
a means of self-expression
as any of the arts.*

–*Fannie Farmer*

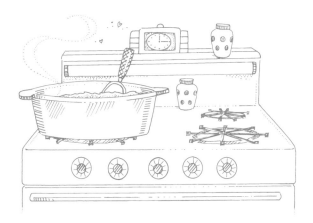

Keep freshly baked bread warm & toasty...simply slip a piece of aluminum foil into the bread basket, then top it with a decorative napkin or tea towel.

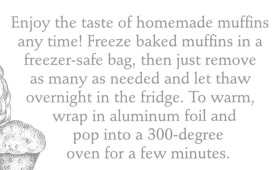

Enjoy the taste of homemade muffins any time! Freeze baked muffins in a freezer-safe bag, then just remove as many as needed and let thaw overnight in the fridge. To warm, wrap in aluminum foil and pop into a 300-degree oven for a few minutes.

Fresh berries all year 'round...it's easy! Just line a cookie sheet with wax paper, spread berries in a single layer and freeze until solid. Remove from tray and place in plastic freezer bags.

Frozen grapes, strawberries, blueberries and cranberries make flavorful ice cubes in frosty beverages. Freeze washed and dried fruit in a plastic zipping bag for up to three months.

Frozen berries can also be used in recipes without thawing.

Don't store tomatoes in the refrigerator...they'll quickly lose their "just-picked" taste. Keep them on a pantry shelf instead.

At the first sign of frost, pick your tomatoes, wrap each individually in newspaper and store in a loosely covered box in a cool, dark spot. They'll ripen slowly and keep for weeks.

Dried celery leaves add homestyle flavor to soups and stews. Save the leaves from celery stalks, spread them on a baking sheet and dry slowly in a 180-degree oven for three hours. When they're crisp and dry, store them in a canning jar. The leaves can be crumbled right into a simmering soup pot!

For thick and creamy casseroles,
try using dry bread crumbs
instead of adding flour.

A handy chart in case you don't have the
exact size pan or dish called for:

13"x9" baking pan = 3-quart casserole dish
9"x9" baking pan = 2-quart casserole dish
8"x8" baking pan = 1-1/2 quart casserole dish

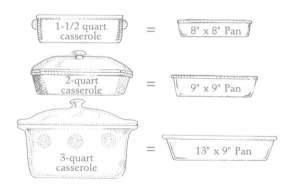

Out of dry bread crumbs for breading chicken or fish? Try instant mashed potato flakes for a tasty, quick substitute.

For a flavorful change, substitute crushed herb-flavored stuffing mix for dry bread crumbs to top a casserole.

Don't toss the bones from a roasted chicken! Turn them
into delicious chicken stock...it's oh-so-simple with
a slow cooker. Combine the bones with a big handful
of chopped onion, carrots and celery. Add 6 cups water,
cover and cook on low setting for 8 to 10 hours.
Strain, refrigerate and skim the fat, then freeze in
one-cup portions. The stock will be ready to use
in your favorite recipes.

Perfect pasta every time! Fill a large pot with water and bring to a rolling boil. Add one tablespoon of salt, if desired. Stir in pasta; return to a rolling boil. Boil, uncovered, for the time recommended on the package. There's no need to add oil... frequent stirring will keep pasta from sticking together.

Pasta shapes like bowties, seashells and corkscrew-shaped cavatappi all work well in casseroles...why not give a favorite dish a whole new look?

To process jars of preserves in a boiling water bath, set sealed jars in a large stockpot and add enough water to cover them by one to two inches. Bring to a boil for the amount of time specified, adding water as necessary to keep jars covered.

Jars of jewel-colored preserves deserve to be shown off! Display golden apricot jam, ruby red pickled beets and bright green dill pickles on a sunny windowsill.

To prepare crispy bacon easily, try baking it in the oven! Place bacon slices on a broiler pan, place the pan in a cool oven and turn the temperature to 400 degrees. Bake for 12 to 15 minutes, turn bacon over and bake for another 8 to 10 minutes.

Garlic is easily minced when you smash the clove, still in the peel, with the side of a knife blade. The peel will come right off, and the clove will be flat and easy to chop!

The true essentials of a feast
are only food and fun.

–Oliver Wendell Holmes, Sr.

Reduced-fat dairy products like milk, sour cream, cream cheese and shredded cheese taste great. They're an easy substitute for their full-fat counterparts in recipes.

Oops! If an unwatched pot starts to burn on the bottom, don't worry. Spoon the unburnt portion into another pan, being careful not to scrape the scorched part on the bottom. The burnt taste usually won't linger.

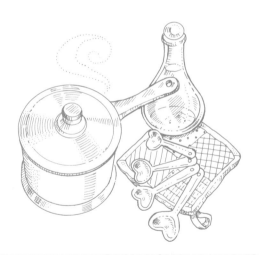

Hot! Hot! If a dish turns out spicier than you expected, turn down the heat by stirring in one tablespoon each of sugar and lemon or lime juice.

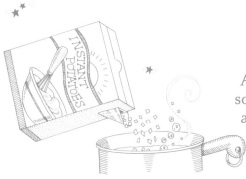

A quick fix for watery soup...thicken with just a sprinkling of instant potato flakes.

Be creative! Change flavors simply by substituting a different cooking liquid. Try your favorite cream soup or replace water with seasoned broth...just use the same amount.

Cook egg noodles the easy way...no watching needed. Bring water to a rolling boil, then turn off heat. Add noodles and let stand for 20 minutes, stirring twice.

Keep hard grating cheeses like Parmesan fresh for longer. Wrap the cheese in a paper towel that has been moistened with cider vinegar, tuck into a plastic zipping bag and refrigerate.

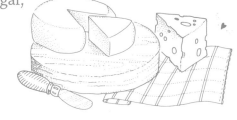

Hard-boiled eggs the easy way! Cover eggs with an inch of water in a saucepan and place over medium-high heat. As soon as the water boils, cover the pan and remove from heat. Let stand for 18 to 20 minutes...drain, cover with ice water and peel!

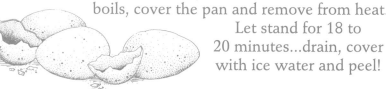

For the freshest flavor, buy spices in small amounts, as they are perishable. Some specialty stores and markets offer spices in bulk containers so you can purchase the exact amount you need.

Take a sniff to test for freshness. Hold the open container at chin height—if you can't detect the aroma, your spice is past its prime.

Freeze homemade or extra canned broth in ice cube trays for terrific flavor when boiling rice. Broth cubes are also so handy when whipping up gravies or sauces for casseroles.

Only using part of an onion? The remaining half will stay fresh for weeks when rubbed with butter or oil and stored in the refrigerator.

To thicken cherry pies, use tapioca instead of cornstarch. High-acid fruits can cause cornstarch to fail.

Did you know lettuce won't brown if you tear it by hand instead of cutting with a knife?

Use white pepper instead of black in cream-based and light-colored soups. You'll get all the flavor with no visible pepper specks.

When boiling corn, add sugar to the water instead of salt. Sugar will sweeten the corn...salt can make it tough.

Did you know when apples are stored in the refrigerator, they'll last up to ten times longer than if left at room temperature?

Lemons will keep three to four days at room temperature. But you can keep fresh lemons up to a month in the refrigerator in a sealed plastic bag!

Bags of salad mix are real time-savers. Keep opened bags of greens crispy by storing in airtight containers or plastic zipping bags...be sure to squeeze out all the air before refrigerating.

If there's no time to make dumplings, use refrigerated biscuit dough! Cut each biscuit into quarters and drop into simmering stew or soup... just like homemade.

Instead of serving traditional dinner rolls, bake up some sweet and tangy cranberry muffins. Just stir frozen cranberries into cornbread muffin mix and bake as directed on the package.

Place a bunch of fresh parsley in the fridge in a water-filled tumbler covered with a plastic bag. It will keep its just-picked flavor for up to a week, ready to snip into soups and salads.

Store your fresh cilantro in a paper towel instead of a plastic bag and it will keep up to three times longer!

Add homespun flair to plain storage jars! Search flea markets for vintage biscuit cutters to fit over the lids and secure with metal adhesive. Perfect for storing summertime herbs, baking staples or dry pasta.

Slow cookers are so handy, you may want more than one! A 5-1/2 or 6-quart model is just right for families and potlucks...a smaller 3-quart one will cook for two and can also be used for dips and sauces.

If there seems to be too much liquid inside the slow cooker, and it's almost dinnertime, tilt the lid and turn the slow cooker to its high setting...soon the liquid will begin to evaporate.

*Spice a dish with love
and it pleases every palate.*

–Plautus

Resist the urge to lift the lid of your slow cooker to take a peek! Lifting the lid lets out the heat and lengthens the cooking time.

It's best to thaw meat before slow cooking, if possible. If you simply don't have time to wait, cook on high for the first hour, then reduce to low and cook as usual... ingredients will rise quickly to a safe temperature.

Keep baking soda on hand for removing soil, wax and residue from fresh fruit and vegetables. Sprinkle a little baking soda on dampened produce, scrub gently and rinse with cool water...no fancy produce washes needed.

A squeaky-clean stovetop...no elbow grease required! Cover baked-on food spots with equal parts water and baking soda and let the food soak right off.

Keep vinegar handy in the kitchen for all your cleaning needs. It removes stains, sanitizes and is safe on just about any surface.

Clean up in a snap! Before you even begin making dinner, fill the sink with hot, soapy water. Put dishes right in when cooking is finished. By the time dessert is finished, cleaning will be a breeze!

Keep cutting boards smelling fresh by simply rubbing them thoroughly with lemon wedges. Works for hands too!

Blend equal parts olive oil and lemon juice to create a polish that will make wood furniture shine. Just apply with a soft cloth and buff.

To clean a thermos, fill it with water, drop in four denture cleaning tablets, and let soak for an hour.

Keep fresh-picked flowers looking perky for a few days longer...add a sugar cube and a spoonful of bleach to the water in the vase.

If your favorite non-stick skillet is sticky, fill it with
one cup water, 1/2 cup white vinegar and 2 tablespoons
baking soda. Bring to a boil for a few minutes.
Then rinse well with hot water and wipe
clean...no more stickiness!

The best window cleaner is a snap to mix up. Add 3 tablespoons ammonia and one tablespoon of vinegar to a spray bottle, then fill with cool water. To really make a window shine, wipe it down with crumpled newspaper!

A quick fix...to clean up spilled oil, just cover the spill with a layer of flour. Let it sit a few minutes, then wipe up with a paper towel.

Before filling a serving pitcher with syrup or honey, lightly coat it with oil. Every bit of what's left will easily slip back into the original honey or syrup bottle.

First aid for old casserole dishes with baked-on food spatters! Mix equal amounts of cream of tartar and white vinegar into a paste. Spread onto the dish and let it stand for 30 minutes to an hour. The spatters will wash off easily.

Try dropping a dryer sheet into soaking pots and pans...baked-on crust comes off in an hour!

If your favorite casserole drips in the oven,
place a sheet of foil under the pan to catch
drippings...clean-up's a snap!

Spilled wine on the tablecloth? For a quick fix, cover the stain with a thick layer of salt and follow with a cold-water rinse. If the stain remains, blot it with liquid laundry detergent, rinse and launder.

Freshen up the fridge! Clean the inside top to bottom using warm, soapy water. You can even sprinkle some baking soda into the water.

Deodorize cutting boards by rubbing with a paste of baking soda and water.

The kitchen is the heart of the home,
and the mother is queen
of the kitchen.

–Owen Meredith

For streak-free mirrors, clean them with rubbing alcohol and a soft cotton cloth.

Rubbing alcohol is also an excellent cleaner for removing ballpoint pen marks from a painted wall.

To clean drip pans and reflector bowls from the stove, take them outside and lay them on several sheets of newspaper. Give them a heavy coating of oven cleaning spray, let sit one hour, and rinse well.

Shine up brass knobs, hinges and fixtures in a jiffy. If they're lacquered, just clean with a damp cloth. If unlacquered, use a commercial metal cleaner...never strong abrasives.

For easy clean-up, spray the inside of a slow cooker with non-stick vegetable spray before adding ingredients.

Even easier...look for plastic liners made especially for slow cookers. Simply toss after cooking!

Take care not to set the crock from a hot slow cooker on a cold surface, and don't fill it with cold water to soak after cooking. Sudden changes in temperature can cause the crockery to crack or break.

For quick clean-up, lightly spritz the outside of a grater with non-stick vegetable spray.

Fill the detergent cup in an empty dishwasher with vinegar, then run on the rinse cycle. A quick & easy way to make it sparkle!

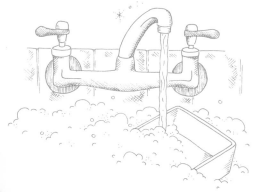

An easy clean-up after baking fish…just pour white vinegar into the hot baking pan and let sit several minutes before cleaning.

An old-fashioned remedy for cleaning copper pots...sprinkle salt on half a lemon and rub the pot. Rinse and wash with hot soapy water and dry well.

To freshen the inside of a microwave oven, pour a tablespoon of lemon juice into a bowl of water. Heat on high setting until boiling and let stand for a few minutes with the door closed, then just wipe clean... no scrubbing!

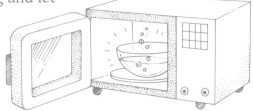

Keep the fridge smelling sweet...tuck in a cotton ball that has been moistened with vanilla extract. A little trick that works with picnic coolers too!

Laundry that smells clothesline fresh and is so soft...with detergent, add 1/4 to 1/2 cup baking soda per load.

To remove egg from mixing bowls, soak bowls in cold water. Hot water will actually cook the egg, making it harder to remove.

If you drop an egg on the floor, cover it with salt, wait five minutes and it will sweep right up!

Get rid of marinara or chili sauce stains in a plastic storage container by rubbing the stain with a damp cloth dipped in baking soda. You can also try filling the stained container with water and dropping in one or two foaming denture cleaning tablets. Wait 20 minutes and rinse.

To remove pesky price tag stickers, run a hot hair dryer over the sticker for 30 seconds and peel off. You can also rub the sticker with a soft cloth dampened with alcohol, or a dryer sheet.

Remove tarnish on silver in no time. Sprinkle baking soda over silver, cover with boiling water and buff with a cotton cloth...sparkling!

Make your own carpet freshener...it's simple! Combine one cup baking soda, one cup cornstarch and 30 drops of your favorite essential oil. Allow to dry. Shake freshener onto rugs, allow to sit for 30 minutes and then vacuum. For flea problems, add 30 drops of oil of rosemary or oil of pennyroyal and brush into carpet. (Be sure to test on a small area of your carpet first!)

No matter where I serve my guests,
they seem to like my kitchen best.

–Old Saying

Whip up a quick & easy valance for a kitchen window...just drape several vintage tea towels over the curtain rod.

Keep a ball of kitchen string right where you need it! Simply drop it into a small teapot and pull out the end of the string through the spout.

A mini photo album is just right for keeping tried & true recipes handy on the kitchen counter. Slide in a few snapshots of happy family mealtimes too!

As you unpack groceries, put new, non-perishable items behind older goods so you know what to use first. A permanent marker makes it a snap to keep everything organized...just write the purchase date on each item as groceries are unpacked.

It's easy to transform any flat smooth surface into a handy kitchen blackboard...try a dustpan or enamel bakeware! Apply two coats of chalkboard paint, taping off any areas where you don't want paint; let dry. What a super spot to jot down kitchen reminders!

Shopping List
1. eggs
2. bacon
3. cheese
4. bread
5. milk

Keep a notepad taped to the inside of a kitchen cabinet door or on the refrigerator...it's an easy way to keep a running grocery list as you run out of items.

Jars of clothespins can be found for next to nothing at sales. Glue them to memo boards or magnets to secure notes or photos.

Keep those take-out menus handy...use self-stick cork tiles to make the easiest-ever bulletin board.

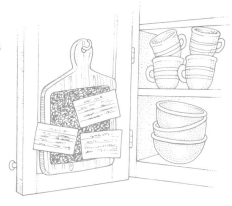

Try this trick for opening stubborn jar lids...just wrap a rubber band around the lid! The rubber band gives just enough friction so your hands can grip the lid tightly.

Love bakes good cakes,
and brews good stews.

–Unknown

Our Story

Back in 1984, we were next-door neighbors raising our families in the little town of Delaware, Ohio. Two moms with small children, we were looking for a way to do what we loved and stay home with the kids too. We had always shared a love of home cooking and making memories with family & friends and so, after many a conversation over the backyard fence, **Gooseberry Patch** was born.

We put together our first catalog at our kitchen tables, enlisting the help of our loved ones wherever we could. From that very first mailing, we found an immediate connection with many of our customers and it wasn't long before we began receiving letters, photos and recipes from these new friends. In 1992, we put together our very first cookbook, compiled from hundreds of these recipes and, the rest, as they say, is history.

Hard to believe it's been over 25 years since those kitchen-table days! From that original little **Gooseberry Patch** family, we've grown to include an amazing group of creative folks who love cooking, decorating and creating as much as we do. Today, we're best known for our homestyle, family-friendly cookbooks, now recognized as national bestsellers.

One thing's for sure, we couldn't have done it without our friends all across the country. Each year, we're honored to turn thousands of your recipes into our collectible cookbooks. Our hope is that each book captures the stories and heart of all of you who have shared with us. Whether you've been with us since the beginning or are just discovering us, welcome to the **Gooseberry Patch** family!

JoAnn & Vickie

Visit our website anytime
www.gooseberrypatch.com
1·800·854·6673

Since 1992, we've been publishing our bestselling cookbooks for every kitchen and every meal of the day! With hundreds of budget-friendly recipes using ingredients you already have on hand, their lay-flat binding makes them easy to use. Each is filled with hand-drawn artwork and plenty of personality.

Have a taste for more?

We created our official Circle of Friends so we could fill everyone in on the latest scoop at once. Visit us online to join in the fun and discover free recipes, exclusive giveaways and much more!

www.gooseberrypatch.com

Join Our Circle of Friends

Find Gooseberry Patch in Your Neighborhood

f Find us on Facebook

You Tube

Follow us on **twitter**

Read Our Blog